SIX DEGREES OF SPORTS

SIX DEGREES°
OF SIDNEY CROSBY
CONNECTING HOCKEY STARS

BY SHANE FREDERICK

CAPSTONE PRESS
a capstone imprint

Sports Illustrated Kids Six Degrees of Sports are published by Capstone Press,
1710 Roe Crest Drive, North Mankato, Minnesota 56003.
www.capstonepub.com

Library of Congress Cataloging-in-Publication Data
Cataloging information on file with the Library of Congress
ISBN 978-1-4914-2143-7

Editorial Credits

Nate LeBoutillier, editor; Ted Williams, designer; Eric Gohl, media researcher;
Katy LaVigne, production specialist

Photo Credits

Corbis: Bettmann, cover (Morenz), 11; CriaImages.com: Jay Robert Nash Collection, 12 (Bobby
Hull), 16; Dreamstime: Jerry Coli, 12 (Esposito), 17 (top), 18 (Orr), 30 (Messier), 32 (bottom);
Getty Images: B Bennett, 24 (Hainsworth), 29, Bruce Bennett Studios, cover (Howe), 10 (top),
17 (bottom), 24 (Hall), 34 (bottom), 36 (Geoffrion, O'Ree, Patrick), 40 (all), 41, FPG, 18 (Shore),
New York Times Co., 23 (bottom), Pictorial Parade, 6 (Morenz), Toronto Star/Barry Philp, 30
(Armstrong), Toronto Star/Frank Grant, 34 (top); Newscom: Cal Sport Media/Evan Pike, 20
(top), Icon SMI/Dustin Bradford, 37, Icon SMI/IHA, 28 (top), MCT/Chuck Myers, 38 (top);
Public Domain: 30 (Day), 35; Sports Illustrated: Damian Strohmeyer, 12 (Jagr), 13, 14 (bottom),
18 (Karlsson, background), 19, 20 (background), 22 (background), 24 (Hasek), David E. Klutho,
cover (Crosby, Lemieux), 1, 4–5, 6 (Crosby, Lemieux, background), 8 (all), 10 (background), 12
(Ovechkin, Brett Hull, background), 15, 18 (Lidstrom), 20 (bottom), 24 (Brodeur, background), 25,
26, 27 (top), 30 (Toews, background), 31, 32 (top, background), 38 (bottom), Heinz Kluetmeier,
36 (Roy), Hy Peskin, cover (Richard), 6 (Richard), 10 (bottom), 30 (Beliveau), 36 (Plante), John D.
Hanlon, 22, John Iacono, 33, John G. Zimmerman, 24 (Sawchuk), 28 (bottom), 39, Manny Millan,
30 (Potvin), Richard Meek, 6 (Howe), 18 (Harvey), 23 (top), Simon Bruty, 7, 14 (top), Tony Triolo,
cover (Gretzky), 6 (Gretzky), 9, 18 (Bourque), 21, 24 (Dryden), 27 (bottom), Wikimedia: 5of7, 36
(Landeskog, background), Public Domain: 12 (Malone)

Design Elements

Shutterstock

J796.962
FRE

Printed in the United States of America in Stevens Point, Wisconsin.
112014   008479WZS15

TABLE OF CONTENTS

REMINDS ME OF . . . .

Sidney Crosby dashes into open space. Like a human rocket, he blazes across the ice. And then it's all about the puck. There on the end of Crosby's stick, the puck dances, glides, seems to vibrate. Crosby swoops in on the goalie, dipping and feigning, and then it's all over so quickly that you're not sure you saw it happen. But it happened all right. The puck is nestled in the back of the net, and the goalie is beginning to pout: It's another goal for Crosby. The fact that you're in disbelief shows that he has done more than just score a goal, though. He has brought you to your feet—or to your knees—and coaxed a roar from your throat—unless he's left you speechless. And whether you say it out loud or not, what you're thinking is, *I've never seen that before.*

But someone has seen it before. This is just about the time your father says, *"Reminds me of Wayne Gretzky."*

To which your grandfather, grin spreading, might have said, *"Reminds me of Rocket Richard."*

Maybe it was an uncle or an aunt who made the comparison. It could have been anyone, right? One element of sports that trickles down through generations is that we love to connect the players of the game. We measure greatness in sports by the records we keep. But we also measure greatness by way of comparison and contrast. We bring together what may be separate by remembering, *Hey, those guys played together for a couple seasons on the same team*, or, *Hey, that guy actually broke the other guy's record!* These types of connections are what this book is all about.

So whether you talk hockey in barbershops or coffee shops, this book is for you. Whether you strike up debate in back rooms, parlor rooms, living rooms, chat rooms, or lunchrooms, on the streets or in the bleachers, with your friends or foes or teachers, Six Degrees of Sports is for you. Enjoy it, and make your own connections.

CHAPTER ONE

WAYNE GRETZKY
Played for Team Canada in 1987 alongside Lemieux.

MARIO LEMIEUX
Owner of and former player for Penguins, Crosby's team since 2005.

GORDIE HOWE
By end of career, owned most NHL scoring records, later shattered by Gretzky.

SIX DEGREES
OF SIDNEY CROSBY

MAURICE RICHARD
"Rocket" had fierce rivalry with Red Wings and their star player, Howe.

HOWIE MORENZ
First superstar of the Canadiens, succeeded by "Rocket" Richard.

SUPERSTAR SKATERS

When it comes to the best players in the history of the National Hockey League (NHL), the skaters who achieve superstar status aren't just the faces of their franchises. They're the faces of the entire league—perhaps the sport. It's as true today for Sid the Kid as it was 90 years earlier for the Stratford Streak.

HEIGHT: 5-11   WEIGHT: 200 lbs.
BORN: 8/7/1987 in Cole Harbour, Nova Scotia
FACT: Crosby scored the game-winning goal in overtime to win Olympic gold for Canada in 2010.

PENGUINS

SIDNEY CROSBY
▶ Center

▶ **Sidney Crosby** attained hockey stardom before he left his teenage years behind. As an 18-year-old NHL rookie, Sid the Kid showed off his superior speed and rink vision as he racked up 102 points. Crosby left veteran defenders reaching in vain behind his perfect assists or watching in awe at his vicious backhanded shots for goals.

Before his second season, the Pittsburgh Penguins named Crosby team captain, and afterward the league handed him the Hart Trophy as most valuable player for the 2006–07 season. Collecting 120 points that year, Crosby became the first teenager to lead a North American sports league in scoring. Since then, Crosby has continued to sparkle. In 2008–09 Crosby helped the Penguins take home the Stanley Cup, and in 2013–14, he won his second Hart Trophy.

Stopping ▶ **Mario Lemieux** was no easy task. He was an imposing 6-foot-4, 230-pound figure and had the skills to score in any situation. On New Year's Eve of 1988 Lemieux scored five different ways: even strength, power play, short-handed, penalty shot, and empty net.

PENGUINS

MARIO LEMIEUX
▶ Center

HEIGHT: 6-4   WEIGHT: 230 lbs.
BORN: 10/5/1965 in Montreal, Quebec
FACT: A three-time MVP and two-time champion, Lemieux scored 100 or more points in 10 of his first 12 seasons.

Not even cancer could slow down Super Mario. Despite missing two months in 1992–93 to treat Hodgkin's disease, he returned to win the league's scoring title with a whopping 160 points. He retired in 1997 and was immediately inducted into the Hall of Fame. Three seasons later, he returned to the ice and played for five more years.

Take away ▶ **Wayne Gretzky's** NHL record number of goals—all 894 of them—and just leave him with the assists. Those 1,963 helpers would still make him the most prolific scorer in league history. Gretzky anticipated plays like no other player before or since and used his soft, puck-controlling hands to turn his guesswork into goals.

The Great One's "office" was the space behind the opponent's net, and he routinely set up teammates with perfect passes from there. The nine-time MVP remains the only player to score 200 points in a season. He accomplished the feat four times.

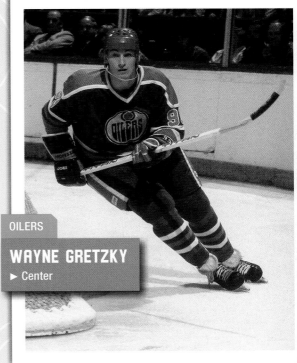

OILERS

WAYNE GRETZKY
▶ Center

HEIGHT: 6-0   WEIGHT: 185 lbs.
BORN: 1/26/1961 in Brantford, Ontario
FACT: Gretzky's impact on the game was so important that the NHL retired his number 99.

▶ **Gordie Howe** was a six-degrees sensation. For parts of five different decades he played with and against the best of several generations. Nobody played more games than Mr. Hockey, whose career began at age 18 in 1946 and ended at the age of 51 in 1980. Opponents feared Howe's elbows and fists as much as they did his ability to score and set up goals. That's why he was a six-time MVP and four-time Stanley Cup champion. At the end of his career, after a short retirement, he was skating alongside his sons, Mark and Marty, with the Hartford Whalers.

RED WINGS

GORDIE HOWE
▶ Right Wing

HEIGHT: 6-0   WEIGHT: 205 lbs.
BORN: 3/31/1928 in Floral, Saskatchewan
FACT: A Gordie Howe hat trick is a goal, an assist, and a fight in the same game.

When he was an 18-year-old rookie, ▶ **Maurice Richard** showed off a burst of speed on his skates that dazzled his Montreal Canadiens teammates. One of those teammates, Ray Getliffe, called the first-year player "Rocket," and the nickname stuck. After blasting off, a rocket has to go somewhere, and Richard went to the goal, where he deposited pucks like no one who came before him. He was the first player to score 50 goals in a

CANADIENS

MAURICE RICHARD
▶ Right Wing

HEIGHT: 5-11   WEIGHT: 170 lbs.
BORN: 8/4/1921 in Montreal, Quebec
FACT: The Rocket led the mighty Montreal Canadiens to eight Stanley Cup championships.

season, setting the standard in 50 games in 1944–45. No one repeated that feat until the NHL added more games to its schedule.

▶ **Howie Morenz** was known as the Babe Ruth of hockey. Just as Ruth became baseball's first superstar with the New York Yankees, Morenz took on that role with the Montreal Canadiens. Morenz's blazing speed on the ice led to several nicknames—the "Stratford Streak," the "Mitchell Meteor" and the "Hurtling Habitant," to name a few. At a time when the NHL played just 44 games per season, he scored 50 or more points three times, including one 40-goal season. A broken leg suffered in a game created complications that led to Morenz's early death at the age of 34. Thousands of fans attended his funeral at the Montreal Forum.

HEIGHT: 5-9   WEIGHT: 165 lbs.
BORN: 9/21/1902 in Mitchell, Ontario
FACT: The "Canadian Comet" was a member of the Hockey Hall of Fame inaugural class.

FACT
Morenz won the NHL's Hart Memorial Trophy in 1927–28, 1930–31, and 1931–32.

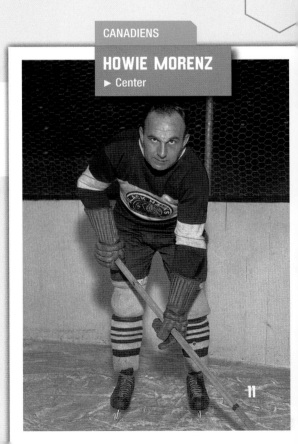

CANADIENS

HOWIE MORENZ
▶ Center

CHAPTER TWO

BRETT HULL
Sixth member of the
700-goal club; seventh
member was Jagr.

JAROMIR JAGR
Played 2001–04 for the
Washington Capitals, same team
that drafted Ovechkin in 2004.

BOBBY HULL
Hall-of-Famer "Golden
Jet" is father of Hall-of-
Famer "Golden Brett."

SIX DEGREES
OF ALEX OVECHKIN

PHIL ESPOSITO

Blackhawk teammate of
Bobby Hull 1963–67.

JOE MALONE
Compiled seven hat tricks in a
season, a feat accomplished
by Esposito.

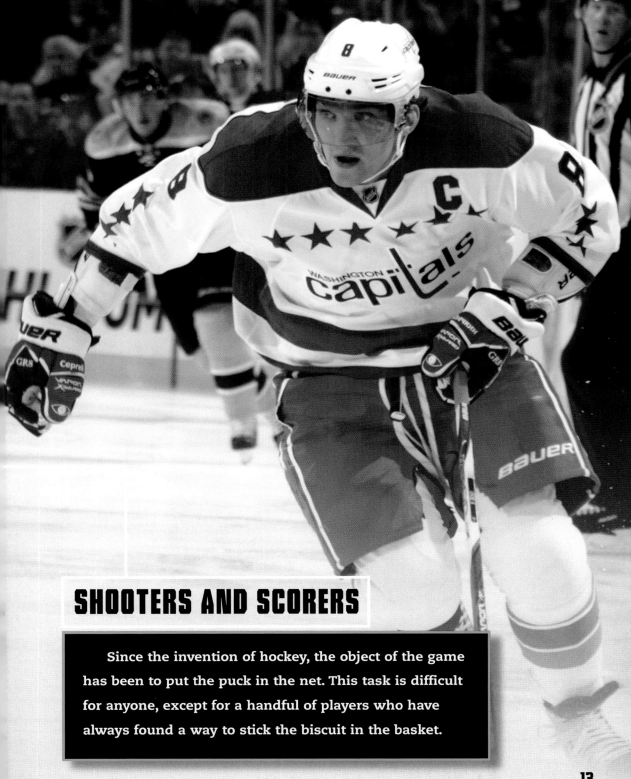

SHOOTERS AND SCORERS

Since the invention of hockey, the object of the game has been to put the puck in the net. This task is difficult for anyone, except for a handful of players who have always found a way to stick the biscuit in the basket.

In 2005 the NHL was desperate for a star goal scorer. The previous season was canceled due to a dispute between players and owners, and someone had to help win back the fans. A gap-toothed ball of energy from Russia would be that someone. Already a superstar in his own country, ▶ **Alex Ovechkin** burst onto the NHL scene as a 20-year-old rookie, scoring 52 times, including one on a falling-down, over-the-head, backhanded shot that to this day is still called "The Goal." Alexander the Great hit the 50-goal mark five more times and won three MVPs in his first nine seasons.

For much of his career, ▶ **Jaromir Jagr** was nearly overshadowed by having the great Mario Lemieux as a teammate. In Jagr's most-productive season, 1995–96, he scored 62 goals, and his 149 points were (and still are) the most ever by a right wing. But Lemieux still had the better season. Big, strong, and skilled

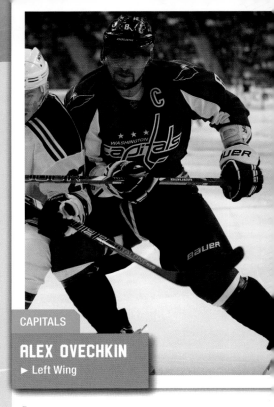

CAPITALS

ALEX OVECHKIN
▶ Left Wing

HEIGHT: 6-3 WEIGHT: 230 lbs.
BORN: 9/17/1985 in Moscow, USSR (Russia)
FACT: Alexander the Great reached 400 career goals faster than all but five other NHL players.

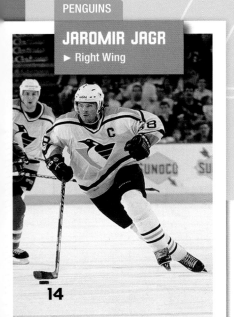

PENGUINS

JAROMIR JAGR
▶ Right Wing

HEIGHT: 6-3 WEIGHT: 240 lbs.
BORN: 2/15/1972 in Kladno, Czechoslovakia (Czech Republic)
FACT: No one in NHL history has scored more game-winning goals than Jagr.

like Lemieux but with a mane of curly black hair flowing out of his helmet and onto his shoulders, Jagr eventually claimed some of the spotlight. He led the league in scoring five times and even passed Lemieux on the NHL's all-time points list.

Every young hockey player dreams of scoring the goal that wins the Stanley Cup, and nothing would be more thrilling than to score that goal in overtime. ▶ **Brett Hull** is one of just 16 players to do that. His goal in triple-overtime in Game 6 of the finals in 1999 beat the Buffalo Sabres and gave the Dallas Stars the NHL championship and sports' oldest and most-prized trophy. It was also one of 24 playoff game-winners on Hull's resume. A true sniper, Hull had nearly perfect aim shooting one-timers from the left circle, especially on the power play.

STARS

BRETT HULL
▶ Right Wing

FACT
Brett Hull led the NHL in goals scored three seasons straight from 1989–90 to 1991–92.

HEIGHT: 5-11   WEIGHT: 203 lbs.
BORN: 8/9/1964 in Belleville, Ontario
FACT: Hull's 741 goals rank third all-time, as does his 86-goal season in 1990-91.

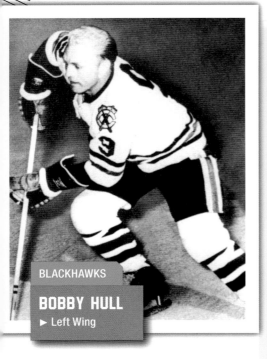

BLACKHAWKS

BOBBY HULL
▶ Left Wing

HEIGHT: 5-11   WEIGHT: 195 lbs.
BORN: 1/3/1939 in Point Anne, Ontario
FACT: Hull's combined NHL and WHL
point total was 1,791, including 907 goals.

▶ **Bobby Hull** may not have been the first player to hit the 50-goal milestone, but he was the first to perfect it. Four of the NHL's first six 50-goal seasons have Hull's name stamped on them. The Golden Jet's blond hair waved in the breeze as he cruised across the ice. And often, that flash of yellow was followed by a streak of black, as Hull fired a wicked slap shot once clocked at 118 miles per hour. Hull starred in two leagues, leaving the Chicago Blackhawks and the NHL for the Winnipeg Jets of the rival World Hockey Association.

▶ **Phil Esposito** didn't mind doing the dirty work. If his battles in the traffic in front of the net resulted in goals for his team, it was worth it. Esposito was known as the "Garbage Man" for mastering the art of cleaning up rebounds and loose pucks and storing them in the back of the other team's net. Esposito was the NHL's first 100-point man and set records that would last a generation. In 1970–71, he

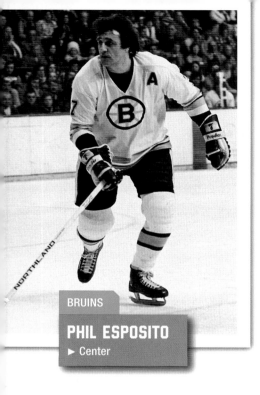

BRUINS

PHIL ESPOSITO
▶ Center

stunned the league by scoring 76 goals and assisting on another 76 for 152 points. He also plastered opposing goalies with a record 550 shots on goal that season.

The early version of pro hockey looked much different from today's game. For instance, forward passing was illegal, which made scoring more difficult. ▶ **Joe Malone**, however, was one player who had little trouble with those suffocating rules. In 1917–18, the NHL's first season, the slippery center regularly outwitted opposing skaters and goaltenders. Weaving his way through the defense, he scored 44 goals in 20 games. Two seasons later, on Jan. 31, 1920, Malone set a scoring record that has never been broken. He potted seven goals that night, leading the Quebec Bulldogs to a 10-6 victory over the Toronto St. Patricks.

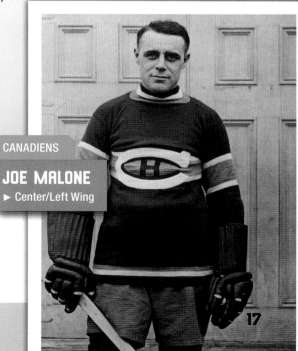

CANADIENS

JOE MALONE
▶ Center/Left Wing

CHAPTER THREE

RAYMOND BOURQUE
Helped new team Avalanche best Lidstrom and Red Wings in 1999–2000 playoffs.

NICKLAS LIDSTROM
Hails from Sweden, same home country as Karlsson.

BOBBY ORR
Bruins stalwart retired in 1979; succeeded in Boston by Bourque next season.

SIX DEGREES OF ERIK KARLSSON

DOUG HARVEY
Won seven Norris trophies, one less than all-time leader Orr.

EDDIE SHORE
Considered NHL's best offensive defenseman, honor later claimed by Harvey.

BLUE LINE HEROES

A defenseman's first job is to prevent the opposing team from scoring. Sometimes that can be done by taking away and keeping the puck. Putting that puck in the net works, too. Erik Karlsson can score and set up goals from the blue line, a heady maneuver popularized by Eddie Shore in the 1920s.

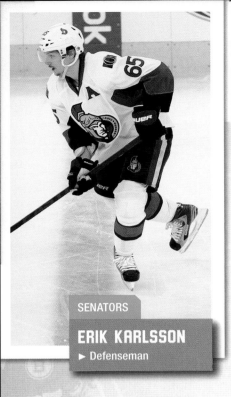

HEIGHT: 6-0   WEIGHT: 180 lbs.
BORN: 5/31/1990 in Landsbro, Sweden
FACT: When he was 21 years old, Karlsson won the Norris Trophy as the NHL's best defenseman.

At first glance, ► **Erik Karlsson** doesn't have the look of a dominant NHL defenseman. He's little shorter than most who play his position—and certainly slighter. But if you're standing around wondering why someone that size is on the blue line, chances are the speedy Swede has rocketed past you and zipped the puck into the net. One of the fastest skaters in the game, Karlsson may be a defenseman in name only. The Ottawa Senators instantly get extra offense whenever he jumps on the ice. In his first five seasons, Karlsson scored 63 goals and set up another 174 scores.

Hockey can be a rough and physical game, but ► **Nicklas Lidstrom's** highlight reel isn't filled with crushing, center-ice checks or big blows along the boards. Instead, Lidstrom used his stick as a magic wand. He disrupted rushes and foiled set plays by blocking, swiping, and poking pucks away from opponents. And he quickly transformed those turnovers

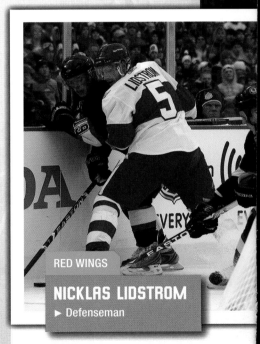

HEIGHT: 6-1   WEIGHT: 192 lbs.
BORN: 4/28/1970 in Vasteras, Sweden
FACT: Lidstrom won the Norris Trophy as the NHL's best defenseman seven times.

into perfect passes to his own teammates. Nicknamed "The Perfect Human," Lidstrom rarely committed a penalty, averaging just 25 minutes in the box per year for his career. The Detroit Red Wings made the playoffs in each of Lidstrom's 20 seasons, winning four Stanley Cups.

When the Boston Bruins retired the number 7 jersey of Phil Esposito, all-star defenseman ► **Raymond Bourque** was wearing that number. Bourque, however, gladly gave up the number and switched his sweater to 77. Years later that number was also raised to the rafters. A swift skater with a sniper's shot, Bourque was a mainstay in the Boston lineup for 21 seasons before moving to the Colorado Avalanche and finally lifting the Stanley Cup that had long eluded him. No defenseman in NHL history scored more goals or assists than Bourque, who finished his career with 410 goals and 1,579 points.

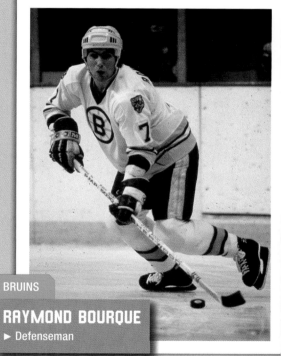

BRUINS

RAYMOND BOURQUE
► Defenseman

FACT

Raymond Bourque was 40 years old when he won a Stanley Cup with the Avalanche.

HEIGHT: 6-0   WEIGHT: 170 lbs.
BORN: 12/28/1960 in Montreal, Quebec
FACT: Bourque was selected for the All-Star Game 17 years in a row, an NHL record.

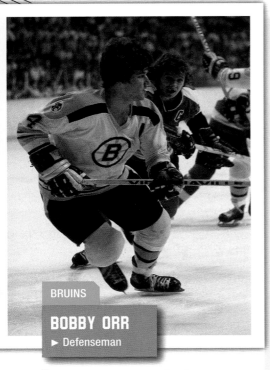

Many talented centers and wingers have clinched the NHL's Art Ross Trophy, which is awarded annually to the scoring champion. Only one defenseman, however, has taken that hardware: ▶ **Bobby Orr**. There had been other offensive defensemen before him, but no one controlled the game the way Orr did. A powerful yet smooth skater, he cruised atop the ice with the puck seemingly strung to the single strip of tape wrapped around the blade of his stick. Skating where no other defensemen dared, Orr won the 1970 Stanley Cup with an overtime goal scored as he dived across the crease in front of the goaltender.

In the 1950s, the Montreal Canadiens' power play was so potent that the NHL decided it needed to change its rules. Instead of serving the entire two minutes in the penalty box, the penalized player could return to the rink if his team gave up a goal. The pristine-passing ▶ **Doug Harvey**, who quarterbacked the Habs' top group, was a big reason for that rule change. For Harvey, there was no better defense

CANADIENS

DOUG HARVEY
▶ Defenseman

than playing keep away with the puck. Once he got it, he controlled it, baffling forechecking opponents with his stickhandling and leaving them to chase his breakout passes.

▶ **Eddie Shore** was hockey's first do-it-all defenseman. The Boston Bruins star defended, scored, and scrapped. He could carry the puck from one end of the rink to the other for a goal. He could just as well slam an opposing player into the boards. And he could fight. When his career ended, Shore had 105 goals, 284 points, and 1,047 penalty minutes. He also had the scars of 978 stiches, 14 broken noses, and several other injuries. Nicknamed "Old Blood and Guts," Shore was the NHL's first villain. He was respected, though, winning league MVP honors four times.

BRUINS

EDDIE SHORE
▶ Defenseman

23

CHAPTER FOUR

KEN DRYDEN
Coached in Montreal by Scotty Bowman, who later coached Hasek in Detroit.

DOMINIK HASEK
First became full-time NHL starting goalie in 1993–94, same season as Brodeur; Hasek was 28, Brodeur 21.

GLENN HALL
Coached in St. Louis by Scotty Bowman, who later coached Dryden in Montreal.

SIX DEGREES
OF MARTIN BRODEUR

TERRY SAWCHUK
Won 1955 Stanley Cup with Red Wings only to be replaced as Red Wings goalie in 1955–56 by Hall.

GEORGE HAINSWORTH
Holder of the NHL's shutout record until it was broken by Sawchuck.

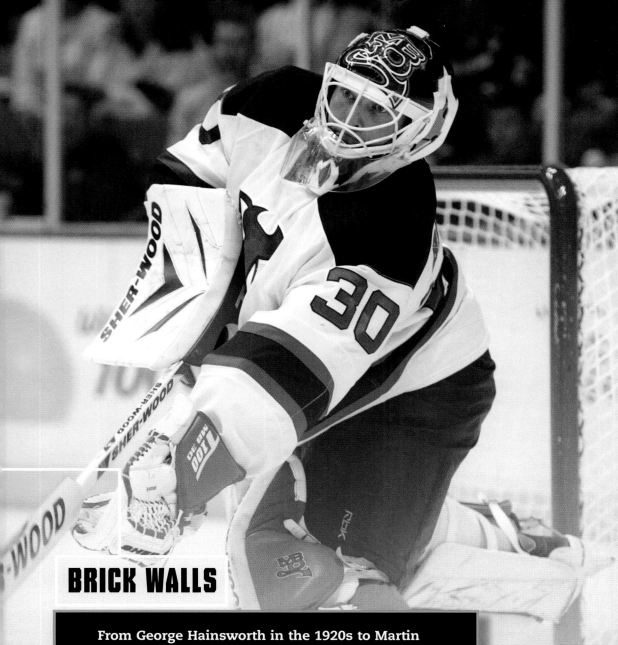

BRICK WALLS

From George Hainsworth in the 1920s to Martin Brodeur today, the job of the goaltender hasn't changed: Stop the puck. The way goalies have gone about that work over the years, however, has differed. They've kept their nets clean by standing up, crouching down, twisting and turning, and dropping to their knees.

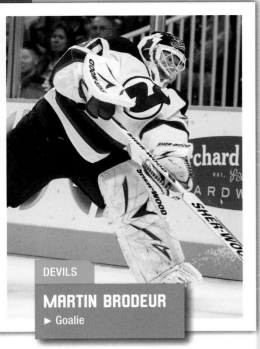

For more than two decades there's been no figuring out the New Jersey Devils' ▶**Martin Brodeur**. Even the best shooters in the NHL don't have a book on him. Some say he plays a hybrid style. Others say he has no style—just a big, athletic body that does just about anything to stop a puck. With Brodeur patrolling the posts by diving across his crease, flailing his legs, and swinging his stick, a gaping net for a seemingly easy goal slams shut in the blink of an eye. Through 2013–14, his 688 career victories were 137 more than the next goaltender.

There may not have been an NHL player more flexible than ▶**Dominik Hasek**. It's said that he was blessed with a slinky for a spine, and indeed his ability to twist and turn and spin and bend turned his net into a miniature golf course for opponents. Hasek would lay out his body on the ice to make one save and then roll

FACT
Martin Brodeur is the NHL's all-time leader in wins, saves, and games played.

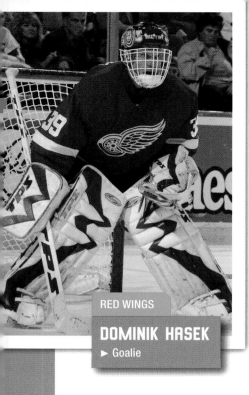

RED WINGS

DOMINIK HASEK
▶ Goalie

HEIGHT: 6-1   WEIGHT: 166 lbs.
BORN: 1/29/1965 in Pardubice, Czechoslovakia
(Czech Republic)
FACT: The Dominator is the only goalie to win two
Hart Trophies as MVP.

and windmill his legs over his head to kick away a rebound shot. No goalie has been able to top his career save percentage, as he stopped 92.2 percent of the shots he faced over 16 seasons.

▶ **Ken Dryden** became a star for the Montreal Canadiens before he was officially a rookie. Called up late in the 1970–71 season, the tall yet quick 23-year-old showed so much promise in his six appearances— all victories—that coach Al MacNeil made the stunning decision to start him in the playoffs. Dryden shined, helping Montreal upset the mighty Boston Bruins in the first round and then take two more series for an unlikely Stanley Cup championship. Dryden won the Conn Smythe Trophy as playoff MVP and the next season won the Calder Trophy as the league's rookie of the year.

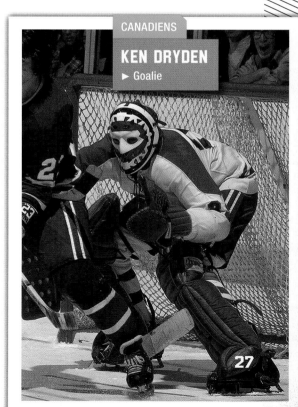

CANADIENS

KEN DRYDEN
▶ Goalie

HEIGHT: 6-4   WEIGHT: 180 lbs.
BORN: 8/8/1947 in Hamilton, Ontario
FACT: Dryden played just eight seasons and won six Stanley Cups for Montreal.

For more than seven seasons, ▶**Glenn Hall** owned his net. No one else was allowed in. Setting a record that likely will never be broken, Hall, the NHL's goaltending Iron Man, played in 502 consecutive games, 552 if you count playoff games, including a Stanley Cup run, in that span. And he played them all without wearing a mask to protect his face! Hall was one of the first goaltenders to drop to his knees and kick out his pads to cover the bottom of the net while relying on his quick reflexes to catch and block high shots.

▶**Terry Sawchuk** played goalie like a cat. He crouched in his crease, his back bent as his eyes scanned the ice and followed the puck through the traffic of players in front of him. He was always ready to pounce. Sawchuk wasn't a goalie who relied on being in the right position. He was a reflex

BLACKHAWKS

GLENN HALL
▶ Goalie

HEIGHT: 5-11   WEIGHT: 180 lbs.
BORN: 10/3/1931 in Humboldt, Saskatchewan
FACT: "Mr. Goalie" had a winning record in 14 of his 18 NHL seasons.

RED WINGS

TERRY SAWCHUK
▶ Goalie

HEIGHT: 5-11   WEIGHT: 195 lbs.
BORN: 12/28/1929 in Winnipeg, Manitoba
FACT: In 1952, Sawchuk had four shutouts as the Red Wings went 8-0 in the postseason to win the Stanley Cup.

goalie. He saw the shot and exploded to it, kicking it, catching it, or knocking it away. The style was more than effective, as he shut out opponents 103 times in 971 contests—nearly 11 percent of his games—and won 446 games.

▶**George Hainsworth's** 1928–29 season might have been the greatest goaltending season of all time. The Montreal Canadiens netminder shut out opponents 22 times in 44 games that season and had a goals-against average of 0.92. Those records still stand today. Even with today's 82-game seasons, no goalie has found a way to beat Hainsworth's improbable shutout record. Efficient in his movement, never flashy, the undersized Hainsworth also played three fantastic seasons with the Toronto Maple Leafs. He finished his career with 94 shutouts and a goals-against average of 1.93, which ranks second all-time. A late bloomer, Hainsworth didn't get a shot at the NHL until the age of 31.

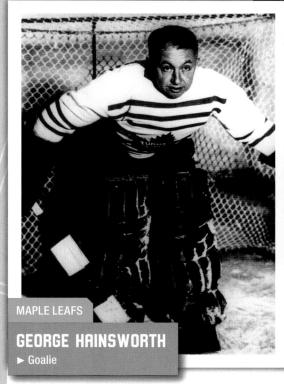

MAPLE LEAFS

GEORGE HAINSWORTH
▶ Goalie

HEIGHT: 5-6　　　WEIGHT: 150 lbs.
BORN: 6/26/1895 in Toronto, Ontario
FACT: Hainsworth received the Vezina Trophy as the NHL's best goalie the first three seasons it was awarded.

CHAPTER FIVE

DENIS POTVIN
Led Islanders in the Stanley Cup Finals against Messier's Oilers in 1983 and 1984.

MARK MESSIER
Won his second Stanley Cup title in sixth full NHL season, the same as Toews.

GEORGE ARMSTRONG
Captained four Stanley Cup winners, as did Potvin.

SIX DEGREES
OF JONATHAN TOEWS

JEAN BELIVEAU
Retired after 20 NHL seasons in 1971, same year Armstrong retired.

HAP DAY
Coached in Toronto by Dick Irvin, who later coached Beliveau.

CAPTAINS OF THE CUP

One of the toughest accomplishments in sports is winning the Stanley Cup. Playing four best-of-seven series, a team must win a total of 16 postseason games to hoist sports' most-prized trophy. Those teams usually have a strong captain, a leader such as Jonathan Toews today or Hap Day nearly 90 years ago.

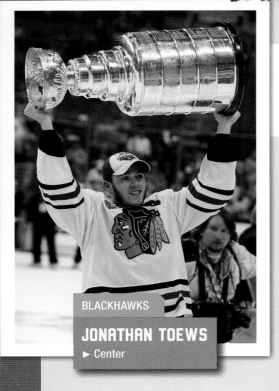

HEIGHT: 6-2   WEIGHT: 208 lbs.
BORN: 4/29/1988 in Winnipeg, Manitoba
FACT: "Captain Serious" is one of the NHL's best two-way forwards, playing both offense and defense.

It was 2010, and the Chicago Blackhawks hadn't won a Stanley Cup in 49 years. Fans in the Windy City were wondering if their team would ever be back on top. A year earlier, the team put a "C" on the sweater of 20-year-old ▶ **Jonathan Toews**, making him the third-youngest captain in NHL history. Could the slick-skating, fresh-faced youngster carry that weight? Turned out, he could. Poised yet passionate, Toews scored 29 points, including seven goals, in 22 playoff games, after which he hoisted the silver chalice as well as the Conn Smythe Trophy. Three years later, he led the Blackhawks to another title.

When Wayne Gretzky was traded from the Edmonton Oilers to the Los Angeles Kings in 1988, it seemed as if it was the end of a dynasty. Gretzky had led the Oilers to four Stanley

RANGERS

MARK MESSIER
▶ Left Wing/ Center

HEIGHT: 6-1   WEIGHT: 210 lbs.
BORN: 1/18/1961 in Edmonton, Alberta
FACT: Nicknamed "Moose," Messier ranks second in NHL history in points.

Cups in five years. ▶ **Mark Messier** also played a vital role on those teams, and he wouldn't let the Oilers lose. In the team's second season without the Great One, Messier carried Edmonton to one more championship. Four years later, he took his blend of speed, power, and passion to the bright lights of Broadway, leading the New York Rangers to their first title in 54 years.

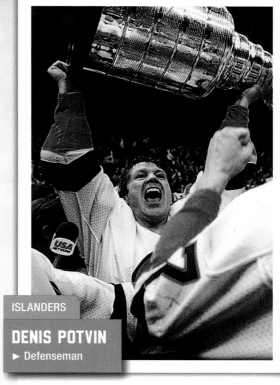

▶ **Denis Potvin** led by example. Whether he was delivering a devastating hip check at one end of the ice or ripping a wicked wrister into the net at the other end, the New York Islanders defenseman forced his teammates to step up their game to match his. Playing with an intensity that had a dash of mean streak to it, he helped turn the Islanders into a dynasty in the early 1980s. With Potvin as captain, the Isles won four consecutive Stanley Cup championships.

ISLANDERS

DENIS POTVIN
▶ Defenseman

HEIGHT: 6-0   WEIGHT: 205 lbs.
BORN: 10/29/1953 in Ottawa, Ontario
FACT: Potvin was the first NHL defenseman to accumulate 1,000 career points.

FACT

Denis Potvin helped the New York Islanders to four straight NHL titles from 1980 to 1983.

HEIGHT: 6-1   WEIGHT: 184 lbs.
BORN: 7/6/1930 in Skead, Ontario
FACT: The workhorse Armstrong was nicknamed "Chief" by teammates and fans for his longtime leadership.

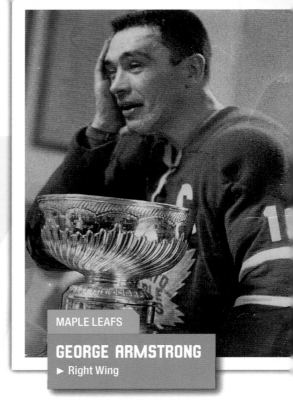

MAPLE LEAFS

GEORGE ARMSTRONG
► Right Wing

► **George Armstrong** wasn't the flashiest player to wear a Toronto Maple Leafs uniform. By today's standards, he'd be called a mucker or grinder. He made his living along the boards and in the corners, battling for pucks to get them out of the defensive zone or to keep the cycle going in the offensive end. So respected for his efforts, Armstrong wore the "C" as the Leafs' captain for 13 seasons. He set a standard that made Toronto one of the best teams of the 1960s, winning three straight Stanley Cups from 1962 to 1964 and one more in 1967.

CANADIENS

JEAN BELIVEAU
► Center

► **Jean Beliveau** was nicknamed "Le Gros Bill" after a French-Canadian folk hero, but he, too, became a hero with the Montreal Canadiens. Big, strong, tough, and handsome, Beliveau was the ultimate team leader for the NHL's ultimate dynasty.

HEIGHT: 6-3   WEIGHT: 205 lbs.
BORN: 8/31/1931 in Trois-Rivieres, Quebec
FACT: Beliveau is one of three Canadiens players to compile at least 500 goals and 1,000 points.

34

A crafty stickhandler blessed with great ice vision, he captained five championship teams, more than any other player who wore the "C." He was the first captain to do a lap around the rink with the Stanley Cup, a tradition today. His name is etched on the trophy 17 times, 10 times as a player and seven more as a team executive.

► **Clarence Day** began his career as a forward for the Toronto St. Patricks. But just as that team changed its name to the Maple Leafs, Day moved to defense. Known for his pleasant disposition, "Hap" (short for "Happy") showed off his abilities as a leader at his new position. Named captain in 1926, he led the franchise to its first championship under the Maple Leafs name in 1932. A few years after retiring from playing, Day became coach of the Leafs and led the team to even greater heights, directing five Stanley Cup-winning teams, including three in a row.

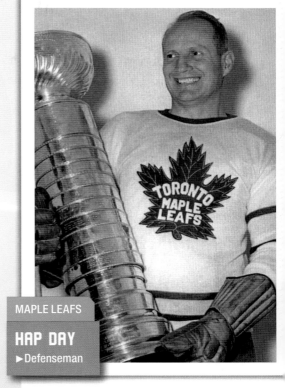

MAPLE LEAFS

HAP DAY
►Defenseman

HEIGHT: 5-11 WEIGHT: 175 lbs.
BORN: 6/14/1901 in Owen Sound, Ontario
FACT: Day and King Clancy formed one of the NHL's first great defensive pairings.

CHAPTER SIX

JACQUES PLANTE
Played first 11 seasons of
career for Canadiens,
as did Roy.

PATRICK ROY
Coach of the Avalanche,
captained by Landeskog.

BERNIE GEOFFRION
Canadien teammate of
Plante 1952–63; also played
for Rangers, as did Plante.

SIX DEGREES
OF GABRIEL LANDESKOG

WILLIE O'REE
In first NHL game for
the Bruins, opposed
Geoffrion's Canadiens.

LESTER PATRICK
Award named after Patrick for
contributions to U.S. hockey
given to O'Ree in 2003.

GAME CHANGERS

The game of hockey has been constantly changing throughout the history of the NHL. For a century, rules have been added and changed, players have brought their own styles and tricks that caught on over time, and room has been made on the ice for players from diverse backgrounds.

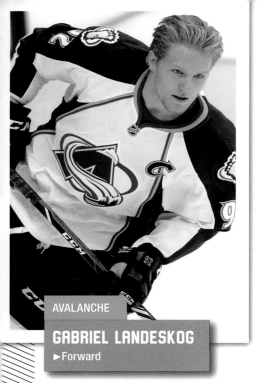

HEIGHT:6-1   WEIGHT: 204 lbs.
BORN: 11/23/1992 in Stockholm, Sweden
FACT: In his first three seasons, Landeskog compiled 57 goals and 134 points.

At the extraordinarily tender age of 19 years, nine months, and 13 days, ► **Gabriel Landeskog** received an honor normally reserved for seasoned veterans and superstars. In 2012 the Colorado Avalanche decided he was worthy—and ready—and made him the youngest captain in NHL history. Described as a natural leader by teammates, Landeskog is a budding star, too. The talented forward breezes by hip checks, leaving defenders to hit air—or worse, the wall—as he goes in on scoring chances. At the other end of the ice, he leads by example, seldom shying away from contact and playing a responsible defensive game.

► **Patrick Roy** wasn't the first player to play the butterfly style of goaltending, but his success with it inspired a generation of goalies to drop to their knees. Glenn Hall

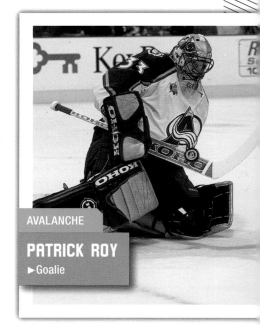

HEIGHT: 6-2   WEIGHT: 185 lbs.
BORN: 10/5/1965 in Quebec City, Quebec
FACT: No goaltender won more playoff games than Roy, a four-time Stanley Cup champ who won big with both the Canadiens and the Avalanche.

was the first to play the style in an era of stand-up goalies, but Roy perfected it. When a shot was fired, Roy's butterfly wings were on display, leaving little room for pucks to enter. Shin pads splayed to cover the bottom of the net. His stick covered the five-hole, the space between his legs. And his big body, along with his blocker and glove, kept the top corners clean. Roy spread his wings for 20 seasons in the NHL, playing for the Canadiens and the Avalanche.

As crazy as it may seem, goaltenders didn't regularly wear face protection for the first four decades of the NHL. On November 1, 1959, the New York Rangers' Andy Bathgate fired a shot that opened a gash on the face of Montreal Canadiens goalie ▶ **Jacques Plante**. Plante left the game but returned with several stitches and something fans had never seen before—a mask. Plante won the game that night, and, despite protests from his coach, he kept the mask on and he kept winning. Plante won the Vezina Trophy as top goalie seven times, including that first season with the mask.

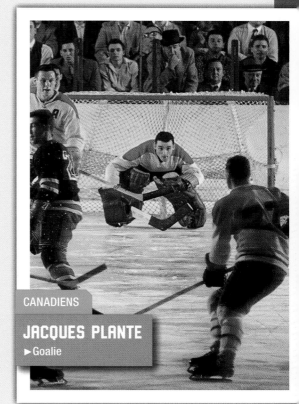

CANADIENS

JACQUES PLANTE
▶Goalie

HEIGHT: 6-0   WEIGHT: 175 lbs.
BORN: 1/17/1929 in Shawinigan Falls, Quebec
FACT: Plante backstopped the Canadiens to six Stanley Cup titles—five without a mask.

HEIGHT: 5-9   WEIGHT: 166 lbs.
BORN: 2/16/1931 in Montreal, Quebec
FACT: The tough-minded "Boom Boom" was known for playing through bad injuries.

RANGERS

BERNIE GEOFFRION
▶ Right Wing

When ▶ **Bernie Geoffrion** entered the NHL in 1950, people were stunned to see him shoot the puck. He had a backswing like a golfer, a windup like a baseball pitcher. And when he swung his stick down to the ice, the puck exploded toward the goal like a bullet. It was the first slap shot, and the sound of Geoffrion's version won him his nickname, "Boom Boom." In an era before goalie masks, opposing netminders were frightened of Geoffrion's rocket shot. He became the NHL's second 50-goal scorer and finished his career with 393 goals and 822 points.

▶ **Willie O'Ree** was a longtime minor-league hockey player who played in just 45 games in the NHL. But they were significant games. On January 18, 1958, his call-up by the Boston Bruins made him the first black man to play in the league. The Jackie Robinson of hockey, as some have called him, played just two NHL games

BRUINS

WILLIE O'REE
▶ Wing

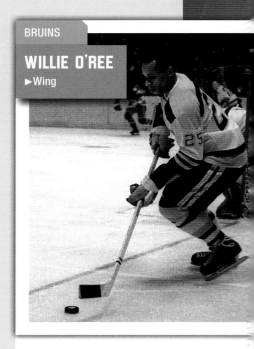

HEIGHT: 5-10   WEIGHT: 175 lbs.
BORN: 10/15/1935 in Fredericton, New Brunswick
FACT: O'Ree won a Western Hockey League goal-scoring title, playing for the Los Angeles Blades.

that season. He returned to the Bruins in 1960–61, when he played in 43 games. He had four goals and 10 assists that season. The next black player didn't take the ice until 1974–75 when Mike Marson played for the Washington Capitals.

► **Lester Patrick** played in just one NHL game. The 44-year-old New York Rangers coach had to play goalie in the Stanley Cup finals as an injury replacement. He won the game, and the Rangers went on to win the title. He coached in New York for 13 years, winning two championships. He was a true innovator, however, founding, along with his brother Frank, the Pacific Coast Hockey Association, building rinks on the West Coast, and writing several hockey rules. Those rules included awarding assists and penalty shots, creating the blue line, and allowing teams to change on the fly.

RANGERS

LESTER PATRICK
►Defenseman/Goalie

FACT
Lester Patrick won Stanley Cups with the Montreal Wanderers, Victoria Cougars, and New York Rangers.

HEIGHT: 6-1   WEIGHT: 180 lbs.
BORN: 12/30/1883 in Drummondville, Quebec
FACT: Defense was Patrick's primary position playing for the PCHA's Victoria Aristocrats, Spokane Canaries, and Seattle Metropolitans.

SIX DEGREES TRIVIA

MATCH THE PLAYER WITH HIS NICKNAME:

1.	SIDNEY CROSBY	ALEXANDER THE GREAT
2.	MARIO LEMIEUX	HAPPY
3.	WAYNE GRETZKY	THE JACKIE ROBINSON OF HOCKEY
4.	GORDIE HOWE	THE NEXT ONE
5.	MAURICE RICHARD	DALLYING DOUG
6.	HOWIE MORENZ	JAKE THE SNAKE
7.	ALEX OVECHKIN	OLD BLOOD AND GUTS
8.	JAROMIR JAGR	THE PHANTOM
9.	BRETT HULL	MOOSE
10.	BOBBY HULL	NUMBER 4
11.	PHIL ESPOSITO	SUPER MARIO
12.	JOE MALONE	ESPO
13.	ERIK KARLSSON	BOOM BOOM
14.	NICKLAS LIDSTROM	THE GREAT ONE
15.	RAYMOND BOURQUE	THIEVING GIRAFFE
16.	BOBBY ORR	KING KARL
17.	DOUG HARVEY	MARIO JR.
18.	EDDIE SHORE	LANDY
19.	MARTIN BRODEUR	MR. HOCKEY
20.	DOMINIK HASEK	MR. GOALIE
21.	KEN DRYDEN	THE STRATFORD STREAK
22.	GLENN HALL	LE GROS BILL
23.	TERRY SAWCHUK	BABY BEAR
24.	GEORGE HAINSWORTH	CHIEF
25.	JONATHAN TOEWS	THE SILVER FOX
26.	MARK MESSIER	THE DOMINATOR
27.	DENIS POTVIN	SAINT PATRICK
28.	GEORGE ARMSTRONG	THE GOLDEN JET
29.	JEAN BELIVEAU	THE PERFECT HUMAN
30.	HAP DAY	THE CAPTAIN
31.	GABRIEL LANDESKOG	UKEY
32.	PATRICK ROY	ROCKET
33.	JACQUES PLANTE	CAPTAIN SERIOUS
34.	BERNIE GEOFFRION	THE GOLDEN BRETT
35.	WILLIE O'REE	THE DOOR
36.	LESTER PATRICK	LITTLE GEORGE

Answers:

1. The Next One 2. Super Mario 3. The Great One 4. Mr. Hockey 5. The Stratford Streak
7. Alexander the Great 8. Mario Jr. 9. The Golden Brett 10. The Golden Jet 11. Espo 12. The Phantom
13. King Karl 14. The Perfect Human 15. The Captain 16. Dallying Doug 17. Number 4 18. Old Blood and
Guts 19. The Door 20. The Dominator 21. Thieving Giraffe 22. Mr. Goalie 23. Ukey 24. Little George
25. Captain Serious 26. Moose 27. Baby Bear 28. Chief 29. Le Gros Bill 30. Happy 31. Landy
32. Saint Patrick 33. Jake the Snake 34. Boom Boom 35. The Jackie Robinson of Hockey 36. The Silver Fox

See if you can guess which NHL team or teams each of the players in our book played for.

Chicago Blackhawks   Calgary Flames   Los Angeles Kings   Hamilton Tigers
Dallas Stars   **Montreal Canadiens**   Washington Capitals
Boston Bruins   Washington Capitals   **St. Louis Blues**   Buffalo Sabres
New Jersey Devils   **Winnipeg Jets**   New York Americans
Ottawa Senators   **Pittsburgh Penguins**   **Detroit Red Wings**
Hartford Whalers   Quebec Bulldogs   Colorado Avalanche
New York Islanders   Toronto Maple Leafs
Edmonton Oilers   **Toronto St. Patricks**
New York Rangers   Philadelphia Flyers   Phoenix Coyotes

LIST OF PLAYERS:

CHAPTER ONE:
Sidney Crosby (one team)
Mario Lemieux (one team)
Wayne Gretzky (four teams)
Gordie Howe (two teams)
Maurice Richard (one team)
Howie Morenz (three teams)

CHAPTER TWO:
Alex Ovechkin (one team)
Jaromir Jagr (seven teams)
Brett Hull (five teams)
Bobby Hull (three teams)
Phil Esposito (three teams)
Joe Malone (three teams)

CHAPTER THREE:
Erik Karlsson (one team)
Nicklas Lidstrom (one team)
Raymond Bourque (two teams)
Bobby Orr (two teams)
Doug Harvey (four teams)
Eddie Shore (two teams)

CHAPTER FOUR:
Martin Brodeur (one team)
Dominik Hasek (four teams)
Ken Dryden (one team)
Glenn Hall (three teams)
Terry Sawchuk (five teams)
George Hainsworth (two teams)

CHAPTER FIVE:
Jonathan Toews (one team)
Mark Messier (three teams)
Denis Potvin (one team)
George Armstrong (one team)
Jean Beliveau (one team)
Hap Day (three teams)

CHAPTER SIX:
Gabriel Landeskog (one team)
Patrick Roy (two teams)
Jacques Plante (five teams)
Bernie Geoffrion (two teams)
Willie O'Ree (one team)
Lester Patrick (one team)

Answers: **Chapter One:** Crosby – Penguins; Lemieux – Penguins; Gretzky – Oilers, Kings, Blues, Rangers; Howe – Red Wings, Whalers; Richard – Canadiens; Morenz – Canadiens, Blackhawks, Rangers **Chapter Two:** Ovechkin – Capitals; Jagr – Penguins, Capitals, Rangers, Flyers, Stars, Bruins, Devils; Brett Hull - Flames, Blues, Stars, Red Wings, Coyotes; Bobby Hull – Blackhawks, Jets, Whalers; Esposito – Blackhawks, Bruins, Rangers; Malone – Canadiens, Bulldogs, Tigers **Chapter Three:** Karlsson – Senators; Lidstrom – Red Wings; Bourque – Bruins, Avalanche; Orr – Bruins, Blackhawks; Harvey – Canadiens, Rangers, Red Wings; Shore – Bruins, Americans **Chapter Four:** Brodeur – Devils; Hasek – Blackhawks, Sabres, Red Wings, Senators; Dryden – Canadiens; Hall – Red Wings, Blackhawks, Blues; Sawchuk – Red Wings, Bruins, Maple Leafs, Kings, Rangers; Hainsworth – Canadiens, Maple Leafs **Chapter Five:** Toews – Blackhawks; Messier – Oilers, Rangers, Vancouver Canucks; Potvin – Islanders; Armstrong – Maple Leafs; Beliveau – Canadiens; Day – St. Patricks, Maple Leafs, Americans **Chapter Six:** Landeskog – Avalanche; Roy – Canadiens, Avalanche; Plante – Canadiens, Rangers, Blues, Maple Leafs, Bruins; Geoffrion – Canadiens, Rangers; O'Ree – Bruins; Patrick – Rangers

43

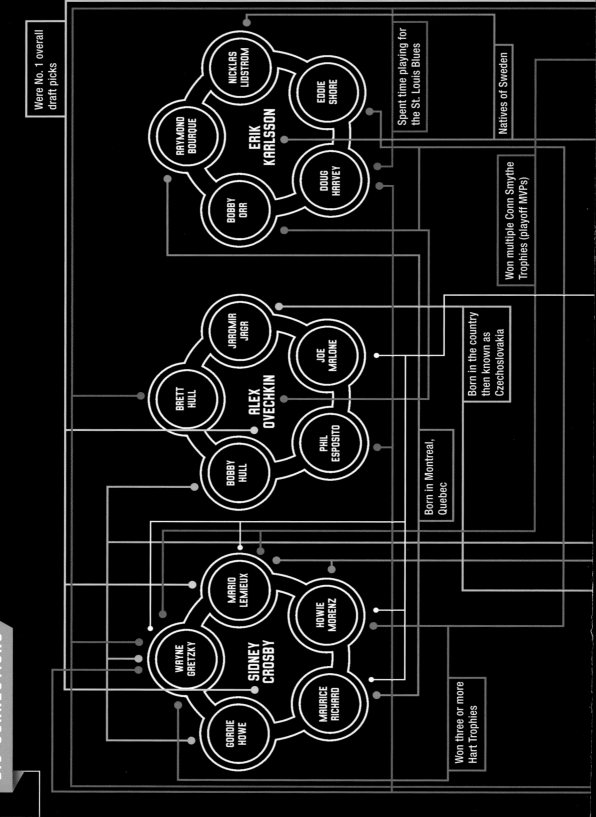

Were No. 1 overall draft picks

Spent time playing for the St. Louis Blues

Natives of Sweden

Won multiple Conn Smythe Trophies (playoff MVPs)

Born in the country then known as Czechoslovakia

Born in Montreal, Quebec

Won three or more Hart Trophies

NICKLAS LIDSTROM

RAYMOND BOURQUE

EDDIE SHORE

ERIK KARLSSON

BOBBY ORR

DOUG HARVEY

JAROMIR JAGR

BRETT HULL

ALEX OVECHKIN

JOE MALONE

BOBBY HULL

PHIL ESPOSITO

MARIO LEMIEUX

WAYNE GRETZKY

SIDNEY CROSBY

HOWIE MORENZ

GORDIE HOWE

MAURICE RICHARD

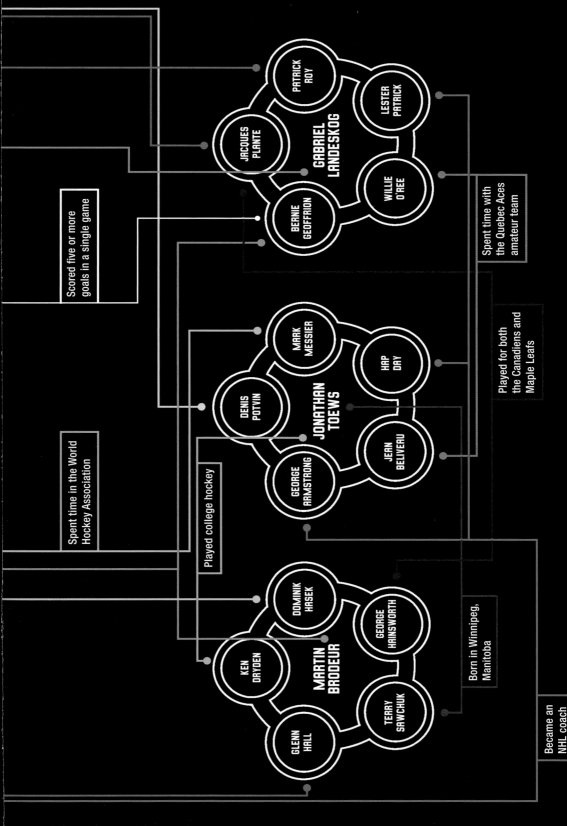

GLOSSARY

blue line—the two one-foot wide blue lines which extend across the ice at a distance of 60 feet from each goal; these lines break up the ice into attacking (offensive), neutral, and defending zones

boards—another name for the wall encircling the hockey rink

forecheck—to check an opponent in his end of the rink, preventing an offensive rush

check—use of the body on an opponent; checking is legal when the opponent has possession of the puck or was the last player to have touched it

crease—the area directly in front of the goal that is four feet wide and eight feet long and is marked by red lines and painted light blue; offensive players not in possession of the puck may not enter

dynasty—a team that wins multiple championships over a period of years

even-strength—when both teams have the same number of players on the ice

hat trick—the scoring of three or more goals by a player in one game

hybrid—possessing two or more different varieties, skills, or ingredients

milestone—an important event or development

penalty box—the area opposite the team benches where penalized players serve time

power play—occurs when a team has a one- or two-man advantage because of the opponent's penalties

shorthanded—describes a time when a team has fewer players on the ice than the other team due to a penalty or penalties

slap shot—hitting the puck with the blade of the stick after taking a full backswing

stickhandling—to control the puck along the ice with the hockey stick

I EAD MORE

Biskup, Agnieszka. *Hockey: How It Works.* The Science of Sports. North Mankato, Minn.: Capstone Press, 2011.

Frederick, Shane. *Hockey Legends in the Making.* North Mankato, Minn.: Capstone Press, 2014.

Frederick, Shane. *The Best of Everything Hockey Book.* The All-Time Best of Sports. North Mankato, Minn.: Capstone Press, 2011.

ITERNET SITES

FactHound offers a safe, fun way to find Internet sites related to this book. All of the sites on FactHound have been researched by our staff.

Here's all you do:

Visit *www.facthound.com*

Type in this code: 9781491421437

 **Super-cool stuff!** Check out projects, games and lots more at **www.capstonekids.com**

INDEX